HOW T
DIGITAL FREE

EXPERT TIPS TO GUIDE
YOUR DIGITAL DETOX

ORIANNA FIELDING

WELBECK

Originally published as *Unplugged* in 2014 and *The Essential Digital Detox Plan* in 2017
by Carlton Publishing Group
This edition published in 2020 by Welbeck, an imprint of the Welbeck Publishing Group
20 Mortimer Street
London W1T 3JW

Text © Orianna Fielding 2020
Design © Welbeck 2020

A CIP catalogue for this book is available from the British Library.

ISBN 978-1-78739-507-7

Printed in China

10 9 8 7 6 5 4 3 2 1

CONTENTS

INTRODUCTION

Technology and media are dominating our lives as never before. Increasingly, we are beginning to feel as if we are drowning under an electronic avalanche of incoming emails, texts and instant messaging. We are struggling with the effects of this continual deluge of digital data and are becoming aware of the impact that being "on" 24/7 is having on every aspect of our lives.

We are living in a culture dominated by digital excess. Many of us, even though we are already suffering from digital overload, seem to be permanently searching for more information, fuelled by an anxiety that we may be missing something – or worse, missing out on something. This "fear of missing out" has been labelled "FOMO".

However, that same technology that enables us to be connected digitally may actually be responsible for disconnecting us from our real lives. While we can feel empowered by our link to a digital global community, that same digital life removes us from experiencing real connections with people in our immediate environment. Often if we are engaged in "real life" offline activities, they are frequently interrupted by alerts from our digital devices, demanding our attention and distracting us from what we should be focusing on.

Studies have shown that digital over-connectivity can also be responsible for causing symptoms of depression and social anxiety, thanks to the lack of real human connection. While our digital life celebrates connectivity, without real meaning and connection our actual lives have no anchor, no core to sustain us.

Our "digital overload" has also manifested another side effect. It has enabled us to successfully avoid spending any time with ourselves. We have embraced the digital tools of connectivity, noise and activity and use them as a new way to live life virtually, instead of actually. Like a new version of the game *Second Life*, but for real people and with real effects.

Take the time to identify if you are experiencing digital overload. Overleaf is a list of the top 12 signs of digital overload. If you find that you identify with more than six of the signs, this may be an indicator that it might be time to undertake a digital detox and reboot your life.

Are you ready for your digital detox?

12 signs of digital overload:

1. Checking your digital device first thing in the morning, getting up during the night to check for messages and regularly using some form of digital device in bed.

2. Slipping away from activities with people in order to check emails or social networking sites.

3. Checking your smartphone while at a meal with others

4. Bumping into someone because you were paying attention to your smartphone instead of looking where you were going.

5. Spending little time outside, rarely taking breaks and often eating at your desk.

6. Finding it hard to complete a task without frequently breaking away to check email or unrelated websites, often checking the same sites repeatedly within a short period of time.

7. Getting distracted easily even when offline and finding it hard to focus fully on one area, or finding yourself unable to switch off your multitasking tendencies even when you're not multitasking.

8. Spending little time in face-to-face interactions with friends. Choosing to spend time online rather than going out, preferring to use Skype or FaceTime to see people, or flaking out on social commitments.

9   Being with family members but spending most of your time at home in separate rooms interacting with screens, often finding that one monitor is no longer enough to suit your needs.

10 Frequently using digital devices to entertain and keep a child occupied instead of talking, singing, playing or reading with them.

11 Going online or using a digital device when you feel stressed or want to avoid an unpleasant task. Using the Internet as a way of escaping from problems.

12 Wanting to stop using your smartphone and finding that you just can't, having tried repeatedly but unsuccessfully to control your social media scrolling.

LIVE

Although our digital connections on one level make us feel as if we are connected, in reality they are not nourishing us. It's like eating fast food, which delivers a lot of calories that temporarily make us feel full, but ultimately does not deliver any nutrition. We are living out in the public domain, presenting an edited version of ourselves. Human beings are much more complicated and messy than can be distilled into 140 characters. To build real relationships we need to understand who we really are. It is a process, one that takes time.

#1
"LESS, BETTER"

Jacqui Marson, chartered psychologist and author of *The Curse of Lovely,* has suggested that the key to connecting with others lies in building better communication with fewer people.

"Try to meet up, face-to-face, once a week or more and bring your whole self and honest experience to that meeting. Leave your polished, edited, digitally-acceptable self at home if you want to feel fully connected, understood and accepted. Which is what, after all, most of us crave."

#2
INTERNAL CHECK

The digital attention we receive can bolster our self-esteem but it also can have a negative impact on how we feel, particularly when the line between our digital popularity and our real-life popularity becomes blurred. Notice how you feel after a prolonged period on social media. Do you feel numb? Do you feel happy? Do you feel bored? Do you feel sad? Acknowledge these feelings.

#3
THINK ABOUT WHY YOU USE SOCIAL MEDIA?

Some reasons are:

- We may be in need of company and find it in our online communities.

- We may be looking to extend our "real world" communities online, enabling further communication to support to our offline activities or businesses.

- We may want to use social media as a tool to find and reconnect with people we have lost touch with.

- We may be living in an isolated location or just feel isolated and turn to social media for an alternative form of interaction.

- We may have difficulty vocalizing our thoughts and feelings face-to-face. Social media gives us all a voice, instantly. We have a forum to share whatever thoughts we have, knowing we will be heard.

- We can use privacy settings to become the guardians of our own experiences, ultimately choosing with whom and when to share them.

- We all want to feel as if we belong and, to a degree, becoming part of an online community, identifying our tribes and joining those groups gives us a sense of being a member of a club where we matter.

#4
GET COMPANY ON YOUR UNPLUGGING JOURNEY

Get involved in an unplugging event such as the National Day of Unplugging. Challenge yourself and your friends, family or colleagues to unplug for a day in the name of charity, or even just for the fun of it.

#5
IS THERE SOMEONE IN YOUR LIFE YOU COULD USE A PROPER FACE-TO-FACE CHAT WITH?

When preparing for an honest and deep conversation with someone, physically move or switch off your devices. Make this a ritual to show the other person how you are giving them your full attention. The greatest gift you can give to someone is your time because that is something you can never get back.

#6
THREE GOOD THINGS A DAY

Connect with yourself by keeping a "Three Good Things a Day" diary. Research shows that comparing ourselves to what we think are others' lives and achievements, as displayed on their Instagram, leads to a lowering of mood, feelings of failure and low self-esteem. First, buy a beautiful notebook that celebrates your intention to do something nurturing for yourself. Then divide each page in half. In the left-hand column, write down at least one thing each day that has made you feel good about yourself, that you are proud of in some way. Then, in the right-hand column, write the personal qualities that this shows you have. This is not as hard as it sounds when you realize you can include all kinds of actions and tasking you might otherwise dismiss: calling a friend in need (kind, caring, thoughtful), cooking a new recipe (creative, daring, experimental) or queuing for a much-wanted item (determined, focused, patient). This is about praising yourself and not waiting for the praise and approval of others. This is a very empowering process and no new technology is required to achieve it.

#7
LITTLE HANDS, BIG SCREENS

If you are experiencing digital overload, the chances are that it is also affecting your family, especially any children who would have grown up with technology. Check here if your child is developing any symptoms of a technology addiction:

5 signs that your child may be developing a technology addiction:

- Demonstrating a general lack of interest in participating in other activities

- Continually talking about digital devices

- Frequent mood swings depending on permitted time on digital devices

- Withdrawal symptoms when their digital devices are taken away

- Using devious behaviour to obtain screen time

#8

EDUCATE BY EXAMPLE WHEN IT COMES TO DIGITAL DEVICES

Children take their cue and learn by copying the adult behaviour around them, observing their parents' use of digital devices in their home environment. Lead by example and make sure that we don't set screen time guidelines for our family while remaining digitally over-connected ourselves.

#9

DON'T WASTE SCREEN TIME ON BABIES!

Studies have shown that infants and toddlers, unlike school-age children, have no idea what's going on when watching a video or streamed programme, no matter how artfully or creatively the content has been crafted. Moreover, the American Academy of Pediatrics recommends that screen time for babies under two-years-old should be limited.

#10
BE PRESENT

Be present when with family members. Listen. Give whoever is speaking your full attention, without holding a digital device in your hand and skimming emails at the same time. Engage with them on their level.

#11
SCREEN-FREE MEAL TIME

Make mealtimes a device-free family time with a no-device rule during meals, to encourage real conversation, enforcing a "no meals in front of the computer" rule.

#12
CATCH SOME ZZZ'S

Bedrooms should also be a device-free zone in order to encourage restful sleep. Turn off or put away screens before bedtime and allow some time for quiet screen-free play or reading.

#13
FRIENDS FOREVER?

Monitor whether your teenager's real-life friendships are taking a back seat to their online social network friends. Talk to them about their friendships or encourage another trusted adult to check in on them and their relationships.

#14
SET TIME LIMITS FOR SCREEN TIME

Making sure there is enough time every day for other important activities, such as schoolwork, hobbies that don't require a screen and spending offline time with friends.

#15
WORK TOGETHER, PLAY TOGETHER

Create a weekly shared roster of family tasks for each member of the family to complete. Reward participation with non-screen activities, for example, visiting a playground or doing a fun activity, arts and crafts time or baking a favourite treat.

#16
GO OUTSIDE

Find an activity that the whole family can participate in. Find a local team or sports club that they can get involved in. If team sports aren't their thing, broaden your horizons, think about life skills that you can invest in with your children that are fun and rewarding. Theatre troops, swimming, music groups, youth clubs all have family-orientated activities.

#17
APP LOCK

Although it feels counter-intuitive to use digital apps to control our digital use, they are actually useful to help us to manage our own and our family's screen time. Parental control apps will assist you in setting limits on your family devices. These apps will effectively control which platforms and apps your child can access and using a time management feature can help you to monitor and track how much time your children are spending online.

#18
PRIVACY IS KEY

New information about privacy and use of our data by service providers is being constantly updated. Learning about privacy and data settings and how they affect you and family should be a priority. Experts have warned about privacy and data breaches on AI voice assist technology and social media. In order to maintain your family's privacy and keep your family's information safe online it is essential to educate yourself on your media providers' privacy rules and how your data is being used.

WORK

One signature trait of our digital world is that it fragments our attention. Our attachment to our computers and hand-held digital devices has led us to view multitasking as our default setting, very often across several devices at once. Rather than view this as a negative, it makes us feel productive and efficient. In reality, though, multitasking actually makes us less productive and has been shown to diminish our ability to concentrate on one thing at a time. But we do have a choice. Our time is valuable and the way we spend it needs to be managed efficiently.

#19
ARE YOU A MULTITASKER?

Rather than view this as a negative, it makes us feel more productive and efficient. In reality, though, multitasking actually makes us less productive and has been shown to diminish our ability to concentrate on one thing at a time. Regular multitasking has been shown to actually reduce our capacity to complete tasks effectively because we invariably end up focusing on the things we are not doing instead of than the task at hand.

#20
THINK OF TIME AS MONEY

Our time is valuable and the way we spend it needs to be managed efficiently. In the same way as we plan how we spend our money, separating it into different areas such as daily expenditure, monthly recurring bills and longer-term savings and investments, the time we spend online across various digital devices also needs to be managed by creating the equivalent of a personalized "income and expenditure" plan for our time.

#21
RELEARN TO "UNITASK"

Unitasking is the process of focusing fully on one thing at a time, immersing ourselves in the task at hand. This means not allowing ourselves to get distracted by the permanent alerts that accompany social media notifications and incoming emails. Allocate a time every day in your schedule to unitask. In the same way that you would schedule a meeting for a conference call, block out a period of time for unitasking. Use this time to focus on special tasks that require your full attention. Select a specific period during the day when the workload is lighter or when there are likely to be fewer distractions.

#22
DECLUTTER
YOUR DESKTOP

While you are working, close all screens that don't relate to the work that you are planning to undertake and open up the one screen only so you can focus fully on the task in front of you. That will minimize the digital distractions competing for your time and allow you to work in a focused and methodical way. Don't be afraid to take up your full screen with one task and close any screens that don't directly relate to what you are doing.

#23
TURN OFF DIGITAL ALERTS

Disabling all digital notifications and alerts for specific periods of time substantially reduces the level of distraction experienced when working online. This will help to facilitate your ability to focus on one task at a time.

#24
SCHEDULE A TIME TO CHECK YOUR MESSAGES

Rather than checking your emails, voicemails and texts continually as they appear, allocate yourself specific times during each day to deal with your messages. This reduces the number of interruptions to the other tasks that you are working on. Another effective technique for managing your email response rate is to add a note to your email signature indicating that email messages will only be checked periodically during the day, pre-empting the need for you to make an immediate response. Alternatively the same message can be sent via an auto-responder.

#25
TELL YOUR COLLEAGUES YOU ARE TAKING TIME TO UNITASK

If you are in an open-plan space, a shared workplace environment or you operate an "open door" policy in your own office, let your work colleagues know in advance that you need to work on an important task and require some uninterrupted time to complete the task at hand. They can be notified when you have completed your work. Book an unused meeting room for some secluded time or request the option to work from home if your living arrangement allows it. Leave your mobile phone in your drawer and focus your attention completely. Your colleagues or line manager can be notified when you are available again.

#26
TAKE AN "UNPLUGGED" BREAK

For those of us who are permanently distracted by the online activity of our desktops, laptops and smartphones, but who find the idea of disconnecting from our online world too challenging, there are apps that will do it for us. They can be set to turn everything off for a period of time which can be specified according to your personal work schedule. Your digital downtime can literally be used as a "breathing space" to take some deep breaths and reconnect with yourself in the real world.

#27
FOLLOW THE 90/10 RULE

The ultradian rhythm, also known as the 90/10 rule, has been proved to affect our energy and concentration levels. Research has shown that to be at our most effective we should change our level of activity every 90 minutes. The 10-minute rest period in between each 90-minute work period encourages the body to go into a "healing state" during which the disrupted ultradian cycle can rest. Rest actively by leaving your desk and making a cup of coffee, visiting a colleague's desk instead of emailing them or stepping outside for some fresh air.

#28
INCORPORATE SOME OFFICE YOGA INTO YOUR DAILY ROUTINE

See below for some examples of yoga that can be done without even leaving your desk.

Office Yoga for Focus

EYE-STRAIN RELIEVER
These two exercises together will relax your eyes and face, clearing your mind and restoring your focus.

Eye Cup
Rub your hands together to create some friction and heat. Cup your palms over your eye sockets while resting your elbows on your chest and bowing your head forward gently into your hands. This calms your mind and soothes screen-tired eyes.

Third Eye Point
Right between the eyebrows you'll feel a bony notch. As you inhale, gently press this point with the pad of your index and middle fingers. As you exhale, release this point. Do this six times. It's a renowned point for alleviating anxiety used in both Indian acupressure and traditional Chinese acupuncture.

SEATED SIDE STRETCH

You can do these at your desk or standing nearby. This brings a fuller, more enlivening breath into your body and oxygenates your blood more effectively, making it easier to focus if you're tired or lethargic.

1   Seated in your chair with feet on the ground, press your hips down strongly and hold your left hand to the edge of the chair.

2   Lift the right arm up and reach over your head towards the left side, stretching the side flank of your body.

3   Breathe deeply and evenly from the bottom of your ribcage and use your breath to expand your lungs and stretch your intercostal (between the ribs) muscles.

4   Do this for 5–10 rounds of breath on the first side, and then switch to the other side for the same number of breaths.

Lisa Sanfilippo,
yoga therapist and teacher

#29
THESE BOOTS ARE MADE FOR WALKING

Sitting for long periods of time has been shown to cause myriad health problems such as heart disease, diabetes and obesity. Combat this by trying to stand for at least part of the working day. Ask for a standing desk, or move around every 30 minutes if possible for a few minutes. Take the stairs instead of an elevator or walk to a colleague's desk instead of emailing them. Follow the 90/10 rule (see Tip 27). This also applies to those who work from home, incorporate regular pauses into your day , try and get outside and take some time to step away from your digital devices and remember to look up!

#30
UNPLUG AT LUNCH

A change of environment, combined with physical activity – whether it is walking to another area of the workplace or actually leaving the area of the workplace for a short walk or workout – will restore energy levels, sharpen focus and clear the mind. Use lunch as a time for you to reconnect with yourself.

#31
INTRODUCE AN "UNPLUGGED DAY" IN THE WORKING WEEK

This would act as a catalyst for creative thinking, face-to-face meetings and group interaction encouraging unitasking and creative flow. Are you overdue a brainstorming session? Are there systems that simply aren't working? An overdue list of tasks being consistently being put on the backburner? Take this day to address these. No matter what industry you're in an unplugged day has a myriad of benefits – think of it as a digital-free onsite retreat!

#32
SET SMARTPHONE BUSINESS PROTOCOL IN MEETINGS

Bringing a smartphone into a meeting can signal to your colleagues that your focus is elsewhere and you are not giving your full attention to the matters at hand. Using a smartphone during a meeting, however surreptitiously, is generally viewed as showing a fundamental lack of respect for the meeting itself and the other people present. If you need your smartphone to take notes, inform everyone present at the start of the meeting that you are doing so.

#33
LEAVE YOUR GUNS AT THE DOOR

Many companies have implemented a blanket "no smartphone" rule for all meetings. One company found a witty cowboy-inspired solution to dealing with smartphone use in meetings by placing a wicker basket at the entrance to their main conference suite, with a sign stating "leave your guns at the door".

#34
ESTABLISH GROUND RULES

Another option is to establish some ground rules prior to the start of the meeting. Ask everyone present to turn off their smartphones or tablets (unless used for note taking) so that they can give their full attention to the matters being discussed.

#35
TAKE A TEXT BREAK

Incorporate "texting breaks" during meetings, to allow participants to either step out of the room at a given interval period during the meeting or to remain in the meeting room and switch on their digital devices for a short period of time, alleviating the need for clandestine smartphone checking under the desk.

#36
BE PREPARED FOR EMERGENCIES

If you think you are going to have to take an urgent call, let the other people in the meeting know before the meeting and set the phone to vibrate. Once you receive the call, excuse yourself and leave the room to take the call.

#37
WORKING FROM HOME? SET BOUNDARIES

Technology has enabled more and more people to work from home, or work remotely. While working from your home environment does have obvious benefits, it is easy to become totally dependent on technology. Setting boundaries around your technology use is essential for your work-life balance and mental wellbeing. Set your working day schedule by turning off alerts at the end of your own defined work day. Being available for work-related matters online 24/7 is not acceptable in the same way you wouldn't be expected to work 24/7 in an office setting. Set up an auto-reply message that gives your working hours and that you will respond to messages within that time. Decide when your workday has ended and take some time out to step away from work-related activities and do life.

#38
SEPARATE YOUR LIVING/ WORK SPACES

Try to keep your working space and your living space separate.
If you can create a dedicated working area this will help you to focus
on work. If you haven't got a living situation where you can create
a dedicated workspace, a kitchen table is just as good as long as
you clear your work material away at the end of the day to mark the
transition from your workday to your home life.

#39
MAKE YOUR BED YOUR SANCTUARY

Keeping digital devices away from the bedroom is key to achieving a good work/life balance which includes digital free, restful sleep. The bedroom should be a dedicated unplugged area. However, if your bedroom is the only space you have to work in then try and create a dedicated work zone even if it's at the end of your bed. Make sure you make the bed and get dressed everyday. Even working in your bedroom, these small rituals will make you feel more professional and productive.

#40
DO NOT DISTURB

Apply the same time management principles to your workday as you would at work by turning off all work-related notifications, limiting the alerts on your digital devices to your working hours only. The "Do Not Disturb" setting on most digital devices will enable you to receive urgent calls only but will disable all alerts and notifications so that you can focus on your home life at the end of the working day. Ideally if you can, turn off your work laptop and store it out of sight.

#41
MAKE AN EFFORT TO CHANGE YOUR SURROUNDINGS AT THE END OF THE DAY

Do something that will enhance your physical wellbeing ideally outside. Go for a walk, a run or take an exercise class. Exercising, even for 30 minutes, particularly after sitting for long hours working on your digital devices for most of the day, will give you renewed energy and vitality. Changing from online to offline activities will also help you to mentally disconnect from your working day and give you a chance to relax and switch off.

#42

AT TIMES, WORKING FROM HOME CAN BE FILLED WITH DISTRACTION

If you need to focus and do some concentrated deep work, although multitasking is seen as a way to increase productivity, research has shown that multitasking actually slows productivity. Unitasking- focusing on one task at a time is a much more productive way to work and can be done from home! As if you were in the office, set your email and key apps to "Do Not Disturb" and either inform colleagues that you will not be picking up on emails or notifications for that time or use an autoreply message.

PLAY

We are becoming increasingly aware that being digitally connected 24/7 impacts on every aspect of our personal relationships. Our connection to our smartphones is replacing our ability to connect with each other. We are now spending increasing amounts of time "together alone", surrounded by friends and family but looking at our smartphones instead of at each other. We also seem to have become an instant "digital response squad", checking and responding to emails, texts and posts on social media as soon as they hit our digital devices, including with increasing frequency during the night and then first thing in the morning – and even, shockingly, during sex.

#43
ARE YOU MULTI-SCREENING?

Whether at our laptops or desktops, or using our mobile digital
devices, we permanently have multiple screens open, switching from
one to the other continually. While it may feel slow and unproductive,
try just doing one activity at a time in a mindful and focused way.
Why not start with just watching TV, or your favourite movie, without
the second screen of your phone? Ask your partner or family to
put away their phones too and watch a movie or TV show together
without feeling the need to react to it on Twitter.

#44
DO A SELFIE AUDIT

Are you living an iLife or is the way you are presenting yourself a
reflection of who you really are? Do you Photoshop or filter your
selfies? Are you projecting an unreal image of yourself? As tempting
as that may be, try going for "real" by posting a #nomakeup selfie,
or moments that actually mean something to you rather than images
that just look good. This could encourage those around you, in your
network and on your feed, to do the same.

#45
HOW DIVERSE IS YOUR FEED?

Does it accurately represent you and your interests? For example, the body positivity movement encourages users to remove any influencers who have clearly Photoshopped their images or who have unrealistic or unnatural bodies and seem to be living choreographed and art directed lives. Feeds and posts that are authentically created because their content means something to you will always resonate with your followers much more than just following and posting the most followed and popular content. Social media algorithms reflect your interests so try to take a mindful approach when you create your profile.

#46

FINDING IT HARD NOT TO CHECK YOUR PHONE DURING CONVERSATION?

Our digital devices don't breathe or have a pulse but we give them more attention than we do the people that we are with. For your next coffee or brunch date, either seek out a café or bar with a no phone rule or make a point of giving the person you are with your full attention by keeping your phone off the table and out of sight. Switch off your data and don't ask for the Wi-Fi password. If anything urgent happens, they can call you. Turn your phone on loud and leave it off the table, in your bag or in your pocket.

#47

FEELING HUNGRY?

According to a study by Brigham Young University, based on 232 people who were asked to look at a large selection of photographs of food and rate them, "over-exposure to food imagery increases people's satiation". They define "satiation" as the drop in enjoyment we experience with repeated consumption. In other words, looking at too many photos of food can actually have a negative impact on our capacity to enjoy our food, because we feel as if we've already had the experience of eating. Co-author of the study, Professor Ryan Elder, describes it as "sensory boredom – you don't want that taste experience anymore". So next time you're waiting for your food at a restaurant, don't scroll through food pictures!

#48
LOVE AT FIRST SITE

When meeting a date from online, staying in public places, communicating via the app instead of sharing personal contact information and creating a special username rather than using your own name will help ensure that these dates are undertaken safely. Some bars and restaurants operate an "Ask for Angela", where you can ask for Angela at the bar if you feel unsafe or your date is not who they say they are. Do your research before agreeing to meet anyone in person.

#49
LOVE OVER THE AIRWAVES

Consolidate all your relationship communication to one place. A new breed of social apps have been developed to provide private online space for couples to share messages and posts. Relationship apps are also beneficial to couples in long-distance relationships or those who have been apart for long periods of time, as they provide real-time connection in a way that otherwise would not be possible.

#50
BLOCK YOUR EX (YES, YOU HEARD RIGHT)

Over 30% of young adults have admitted to either monitoring the posts, photos and relationship status of an ex-partner or posting photos and status updates specifically designed to make their ex jealous. Don't be that person, hide them from your timeline or block them completely. If you don't have the strength to do it yourself hand your device over to a trusted friend and have them purge your socials of all temptation.

#51
TOO MANY FISH IN THE SEA?

Although dating sites and apps provide access to a huge volume of potential partners, the enormous amount of prospective matches can be overwhelming and lead us to suffer from "choice overwhelm". This can drive people to make misjudged choices through having too many options available to them and discourage commitment thinking that someone better will appear on their next search.

#52
WATCH OUT FOR RABBIT HOLES

"Falling down a rabbit hole" is a term for intending to spend a short amount of time to look up something or check an email and finding yourself having spent hours on low value online activities such as surfing, social media and online shopping. As Alice in Wonderland knows, it may be tempting to buy into the online fantasy, but be aware that the culture of instant gratification. While buying something we don't need or spending five hours on YouTube can give us a temporary dopamine rush, it is not worth it in the long term.

#53
CHECK OUT YOUR CART

Digital payment apps such as Google Pay and Apple Pay have encouraged frequent shopping online. With "buy now pay later" apps like Klarna encouraging buying more of what you can't always afford, some simple techniques can help you to manage your shopping habits. The fact we like something (we like a lot of things) doesn't mean we have to buy it. Before you click "Buy", pause and ask yourself: do I need this? Will I use it? How often will I wear this? Will it last? The answer to most of your questions will be "No" You can help yourself to shop online in a more considered way by removing your card details from your usual shopping sites and clearing your card information from your cached data.

#54
WE ALL SUFFER FROM INBOX OVERLOAD

One way to manage unnecessary marketing and junk emails is to invest some time unsubscribing from as many of them as you can. You'll be surprised much more streamlined and manageable your inbox will become! Another method is to have a secondary email account that you only use for emails that you subscribe to, that way those emails will be automatically filtered into your other account inbox and will leave more space in your main inbox for your work and important emails.

#55
PROTECT YOUR INFORMATION

It is also very important to remember that when using public Wi-Fi outside of the home or work environment try and avoid giving any kind of personal information online and be aware of your surroundings. Avoid using public Wi-Fi when making purchases online or using online banking. Being vigilant will assist you in better protecting your personal information and prevent anyone from intercepting your email, cloning your card details or using your bank details to make unauthorized purchases.

#56
DITCH THE FITBIT

While fitness apps are great motivators to go outside and get exercising, counting your steps and competing with your friends' fastest run times actually distract you from the real purpose of exercise – to reconnect with your body and your surroundings. Turn your phone onto airplane mode and put it away so that you can focus on your breath and your body. Disconnecting for a while will help you to be present and consciously enjoy the scenery.

#57
EXERCISE MINDFULLY

Make a conscious effort to unplug during exercise so that you can concentrate on how you feel and the way your body is responding to that particular form of exercise. Monitor your energy levels and your breathing pattern.

Some forms of exercise are great to do on your own such as yoga or Pilates. Going for a walk or a run can also be a form of mindful exercising if done by yourself but it can also be a more of a social activity and provide the perfect opportunity to meet up and exercise with a friend.

#58
STREAMING: THE ANALOGUE WAY

Over the past few years vinyl has made a comeback as a more purist form of listening to music. According to vinyl enthusiasts, it is a much more physical experience than streaming which makes it the perfect way to listen to music while digitally unplugging. Playing vinyl on a record player is a much more connected and immersive experience. If you don't have access to a record player try using a CD player to listen to some throwback sounds.

#59
GETTING ALL YOUR INFORMATION FROM YOUR NEWSFEED?

Newsfeeds are algorithmically driven to reflect your likes and interests so often are like an echo chamber feeding you information about things you already have an interest in. To get a more balanced view try changing your news sources and go analogue by buying newspapers and subscribing to magazines. This will gives you a chance to unplug from your constant digital newsfeeds and get a broader and more balanced view of the world.

PAUSE/
DISCONNECT

In order to be able to take a step back and think about the way we use our digital devices – and the way they are both using and losing us – we need to disconnect. We can decide to change the way we live and take those first steps towards a life that enables us to be the best version of ourselves. Every day, we can do one thing that will take us forward to where we want to be. Instead of allowing technology to control our lives, we can learn to access our "inner technology" and find new ways to live deliberately, consciously and mindfully. Unplugging enables us to recharge the mind, body and soul.

#60
CONNECT YOUR HEAD AND YOUR HEART

Psychologists, such as Jacqui Marson, often recommend mindfulness. It is scientifically proven that mindfulness can have a positive effect on our health and emotional wellbeing. As Marson explains, "It is important to take time to unplug from the digital, visual world and reconnect with the rest of our senses. Mindfulness gives us some very simple ways to start. When you have your first cup of tea or coffee of the day, take the time to really taste it. Bring the attention of your busy mind to the feeling of the hot liquid in your mouth, the texture on your tongue, the aromas of the steam. When you shower, wash your hands or brush your teeth, focus on the sensations, the sounds of the water rushing, the feeling of it on your skin. By taking the opportunity to develop new habits of mindful awareness with these everyday tasks, we can begin to reawaken all five senses and reconnect with the world, ourselves and others, and start to balance the visual tyranny of the digital world."

#61
FIND YOUR NATURAL SPACE

Unplugging is not just about rejecting or parking our digital devices. It is about being in a both mental and physical space that allows us to recharge and reconnect with the natural rhythm of life and gain new perspective on our relationship with ourselves and with the technology we use. Find your natural space — inside and out.

#62
MEDITATE

Meditation is not a "quick fix" practice. It is a slow, continual, self-motivated discipline to enable us to reconnect with our inner being. See overleaf for the first steps on your personal meditation journey.

In order to start meditating, there are six basic things you can do to prepare yourself that apply whichever type of meditation practice you decide to follow:

1   **Make a sanctuary space.** Find a quiet place that you connect with, which has few distractions and where you will not be interrupted. This could be a special corner of a room, a bench in the garden, a comfortable armchair or a favourite rug, anywhere that can become your special place, where you can find a peaceful "pause".

2   **Find your position.** Try out a few seated positions until you find the one you are most comfortable in and are able to remain in for the duration of your meditation. Meditation is mostly practised in a seated position to avoid the risk of falling asleep, but depending on the type of meditation you can practise lying down, standing or even walking.

3   **Shhhhhh ...** Prior to meditating, in order to bring a quietness to your mind, it can be helpful to sit in silence, focusing on your breath until your heartbeat slows down.

4   **Centre your focus.** Focusing the attention forms an intrinsic part of meditation practice. Usually, this will be on your breath, on a mantra (a phrase or sequence of words) or on a specific object. In other types of meditation you will concentrate on whatever thoughts dominate your consciousness.

5   **Let it be.** In meditation it is conducive to try to view your mind as an "impartial observer" by letting thoughts and distractions come and go naturally without judging them. When we find our attention wandering, rather than overriding them by trying to suppress them, we gently bring our attention back to the centre of our focus, objectively observing our thoughts and emotions.

6   **Small steps.** At the beginning of your meditation journey, it is important to remember meditation is a process. Meditation does not have a destination, so the setting of personal challenges such as meditating for a specific length of time or reaching the "peace spot" are a complete antithesis to the essence of the practice. As meditation becomes more integrated with your daily life, the length of practice will gradually increase naturally and without requiring conscious effort. Over time, you will find that you can meditate whenever you wish and wherever you are.

#63
GET IN THE ZONE

In order to generate some space between ourselves and our digital devices, we need to create mental and physical zones in our life that are unplugged. Digital downtime, through yoga, meditation or another physical or creative activity, enables us to integrate the different spaces in our lives and start to live life to the fullest potential. Look at your daily routine or daily schedule. Is there any place that you can begin to practise the separation between your digital time and me time. Is it first thing in the morning? On your lunch hour? Just before bed? Make a mindful effort to carve out time for your digital-free zone.

#64

MAKE A DIGITAL-FREE SANCTUARY

Select a space in the home, a room ideally, if not a chair or a quiet corner. Fill it with plants and soft fabrics, dimmed lights and dedicate this space as your breathing space away from technology. Do yoga, meditate, read, write or listen to music to create a digital-free space. Set a timer on your phone and put it out of reach. Challenge yourself to sit in this space and focus on doing nothing for a period of time. Eventually lengthen that period of time to see how little time you need to give your phone.

#65

TAKE UP YOGA

Yoga is a holistic practice that integrates meditation, breathing and movement to harmonize all the elements that make us who we are. See overleaf for an introduction to the core tenet of yoga – the balancing breath.

BALANCING BREATH

Increase your focus by calming and balancing the nervous system, decreasing mental tension, and connecting to your physical and mental centre. Breathing with an even inhalation and exhalation balances the activating and relaxing parts of the autonomic nervous system. This basic yoga breath is subtle enough to do anywhere, any time, when you are feeling stressed or tense, or have a buzzing brain.

To learn this, start by making a whispery "haaah" sound – breathing out with a gentle constriction at the back of the throat.

1   Place your palm in front of your mouth and pretend it's a mirror; use your breath as though you're going to fog it up.

2   Next make the same "haaah" that tones the back of the throat as you breathe out with your mouth closed.

3   Breathe through your nose keeping the tone in the back of your throat. Now try the tone in your throat as you inhale.

4. Continue inhaling and exhaling with that tone in the throat that lengthens your breath. Breathe deeply and comfortably into your lungs, as though filling the bottom back part of your lungs with air as you breathe.

5. Your inhale and exhale should be the same length by counting: inhale-two-three then a gentle pause, then exhale-two-three. It may take some practice to get your breath to feel fluid, without any pauses or jagged stops during the in-breath or out-breath.

If you find the breath "catches", this is a sign to soften your throat so you can breathe smoothly into your lungs. It's important to focus on filling the whole of your lungs, and keep the tone in the throat very soft, so that it is just a marker of the breath and doesn't create any additional tension.

Lisa Sanfilippo,
Yoga Therapist and Teacher

#66
BOOK A RETREAT

When booking a retreat or a holiday, consider a digital detox camp. If the idea of "going it alone" is too challenging, there are an increasing number of spas and wellness retreats that will guide you through the process.

#67
YOUR TRIBE IS OUT THERE

Find communal activities that keep both of your hands busy Growing things, crafting, cooking, sports – all of these can be social as well as practical events. Who knows? You might even have experiences and meet people that you never would have encountered through a screen.

#68
EMBRACE "THE ART OF SLOW"

The art of slow is about creating space without the need to fill it. The "slow" philosophy is much more about finding a way of doing everything at its own natural pace, in the best way you can. It focuses on the quality rather than quantity of what you are doing. Overleaf are 16 simple ways to pause and embrace the "art of slow":

1   Be silent. Give your mind some space.

2   Breathe consciously (see Balancing Breath, page 72).

3   Find time to meditate.

4   Spend some quiet time alone.

5   Write down your thoughts and ideas.

6   Draw, paint or make something.

7   Sing or make music, alone or in a group.

8   Walk everywhere, as often as you can. Instead of getting a drive-by coffee from a multinational chain, walk to your nearest independent café and build a relationship with your barista.

9   Discover what your neighbourhood has to offer by walking or cycling there and explore the richness and variety of local shops and markets.

10 Smile at a stranger. It doesn't cost you anything but that moment of connection may just make their day and yours!

11 Talk to others.

12 Go to a park you have always driven past but have never stopped at.

13 Immerse yourself in nature and wildlife. Visit a bird sanctuary, national park or hiking trail.

14 Source locally grown produce at local farmers' markets instead of pushing a metal trolley around a brightly lit supermarket. This supports your local community and the environment and goes a long way to helping you reconnect with your neighbourhood.

15 Find out about the provenance and backstory of your "farm to table" food. This will establish a connection between you and the grower, fundamentally changing the way you experience the eating of that produce.

16 Grow something from seed. The process of planting a seed and watching it grow through constant care and nurturing is the perfect analogy for living a slower, more connected and authentic life. We cannot hurry nature – everything happens in its own time. In the same way, if we connect with the natural rhythms of our world and respect them rather than trying to manipulate and control them to fit in with our digitally determined schedules, we will find that we do not have to stop moving in order to slow down; we just have to relearn how to move in a different, and more meaningful, way. We simply have to be able to pause for long enough to notice the details that shift our lives from the manic to the micro.

RECONNECT

Our world is complex, overloaded and overwhelming. Increasingly we are finding that we need to step back from the tsunami of excessive information that being permanently online creates. We need to pause for long enough in a space free from digital overload to be able to find presence and be able to reconnect with the inherent rhythm of life. This will gradually enable us to find the place in ourselves where we are, and give ourselves permission just to "be". Change your "to do" list for a "to be" list with these mindful steps.

#69
BREATHE

We breathe unconsciously all the time. Even if we don't consciously make the effort to breathe, we still breathe. So if we make a conscious effort to concentrate fully on our breath, it is one of the purest, most balancing and life-enhancing things we can do and is fundamental to our wellbeing. So whenever you can, take a few minutes away from your digital life and allow stillness in. Feel your breath. Focus on breathing in slowly and breathing out even more slowly. Breathe consciously. Take three deep breaths every hour throughout the day. Embrace the rhythm of your breath like the sound of the wind or of gentle waves. Find your special space; your inner happy place that is always there with every breath.

#70
LOOK UP

We can't experience the light and dark of life through a two-inch backlit screen. Remember that above us is a huge, expansive sky. Ever-changing. Always there. Looking up gives us context and helps us to regain a more balanced perspective and remember to explore the outer edges of life. Even if you can only take five minutes to look at the sky through a window, take those five minutes for you. Watch the clouds, focus fully on the changing shapes, look at the shadows they cast. Be present. Those five minutes are always there for you to take on a "need to slow" basis.

#71
ALLOW THE "NOW"

Simone Weil wrote: "Attention is the rarest and purest form of generosity." Now is all there is. When we fully concentrate on being in the "now", we are free. Free of "what if", "I should have" and "I wish I could". They don't exist. Yesterday doesn't exist any more. Tomorrow hasn't arrived. All we have is now. So if we can focus fully on this moment right now, it is the purest form of being. It simplifies everything. Whether you are doing something, going somewhere or talking to someone, be there, be present, be at one with yourself and be secure in the knowledge that where you are right now is exactly where you are meant to be.

#72
GET OUT MORE

See a tree. Think outside. No box required. Being immersed in our digitally connected world mostly means that we are living inside our heads and inside buildings. Our bodies and our senses are starved of attention and are suffering from abandonment anxiety. It is so easy to forget that the body directs traffic. It is where everything is housed; it is our very own mainframe computer. Yet we seem to have to continually remind ourselves to physically reconnect with our bodies. We just have to get out more. Recent studies have shown that we need to change our level of activity every 90 minutes. Sitting for extended periods has been shown to be seriously detrimental to your health. Even if it is only for a 10-minute break, leave your smartphone behind, take a walk, focus fully on what you see. This will encourage a new dialogue between the brain and the body, allowing the mind to relax and decompress enough to give it the space to connect with our emotions. Even without having an overtly natural environment around you, the act of walking outside mindfully, getting your body moving, experiencing a change of scenery, focusing on a new backdrop, concentrating on the increase in energy that you feel, will restore balance to your system and provide an effective pause for your digitally-overloaded mind.

#73
UNITASK

What we do matters. How we do it matters more. You have already applied the concept of unitasking at work, now bring it into your everyday life. Given our extreme multitasking tendencies, working over several platforms and various screens at the same time, many of us are actually finding that we are losing our ability to concentrate on one thing at a time. When we do one thing at a time it can feel slow and unproductive. In fact, concentrating fully and in a focused way on one task increases productivity. Research shows that the effects of multitasking result in us having trouble focusing and filtering information, and lead to increased stress levels. It has further been shown that even when we have finished our multitasking activity, the residual effects of our fractured thinking and lack of focus stays with us for an extended period.

#74
IT'S INTENTIONAL

Establish your intention for the day. By starting the day with a single prioritized focus, this will encourage concentration and create a manageable guide for your day's activities. Ask yourself what you would like to achieve during this day and what quality you want to embody while you are moving towards your intention. We are generally so focused on trying to do as much as we can that we often forget to concentrate on the quality of the individual tasks we are actually undertaking, and the way we are while we are completing them.

#75
FACETIME: THE ANALOGUE VERSION

As human beings, we have a primal need to touch and feel and connect in a real way. We have to remember that within us is a fundamental human desire to feel emotion face-to-face and not just through a digital filter. It is important to engage our five senses again and start to touch things other than a digital device. We thrive on facial feedback, as emotionally this gives us a sense of wellbeing through oxytocin being released by the brain. We need to stop finding ways, through digital distraction, to avoid physical contact.

#76
MINDSET RESET

Find your own "mindset reset" button. Try to spend at least five minutes each day doing nothing; ideally several times a day. First thing in the morning, instead of reaching for your smartphone, checking your emails and scanning through your mental to-do list, try to spend five minutes with your eyes shut practising gratitude for all the things in life that you have, that money can't buy. There is no limit to the practice of gratitude; you can fit in a quick five-minute "mindset reset" anytime, anywhere. **Express gratitude, live in possibility, stay curious and be generous.**

YOUR
DIGITAL
DETOX

Are you ready to digitally detox? Level up your detox, from a one-hour tech-free taster to the equivalent of a seven-day "Unplug and Play" vacation. Begin with steps 77–87 to prepare for and support your digital detox. Each of us is unique, therefore there is no "one size fits all" solution. The idea is to provide a "pick and mix" selection that you can undertake according to your schedule and lifestyle. The detoxes can be done in sequence, undertaken individually, or combined to create a personalized plan that works for you.

#77
STARTING BRIEF

Take a pen and paper and find a quiet space, ideally with a table and chair where you can be on your own for 30 minutes. Take a few minutes to focus fully on your life and how it is now. **Now imagine for a moment that this was your last day**. Take some time to really think about and then **write a list of the 10 most important things** that you would want to do with your last day.

Think about your last day. Would you want to clear your inbox by answering every one of the 500 pending emails waiting for you there? Would sending that tweet and Instagramming that meal and checking into Facebook be your priority? Or would you give anything to actually be able to touch, hug and talk face-to-face with a loved one? Or go for a walk surrounded by nature? Or go and visit the people and places you love, in person? **We don't have to wait until it's too late. Choose life now.**

#78
ON POINT

Focus fully on your life and think about what you would like to achieve during your digital detox and write down your goals in your notebook. Establishing a set of personal goals that are achievable will encourage you and provide you with an incentive to continue with the digital detox plan until you have reached these goals.

They could be larger life goals such as spending your newly available "unplugged" quality time with friends and family or starting to pursue a long-held passion, or they could be more practical such as taking your smartphone out of the bedroom at night, or deciding to only check your email once a day at the weekend, or a combination of both. Committing your goals to paper will give your digital detox a focus and will provide an effective guide to keep you on track to achieving your detox goals. Once written down you can carry your notebook with you and refer to your list of goals on a "need to" basis.

#79
WRITE IT OUT

Keeping a daily detox diary will enable you to monitor your progress and provide you with a valuable record of your digital detoxing journey. Be honest with yourself and include any obstacles that you come across, whether self-generated or due to external circumstances, so that they can be highlighted, reviewed and addressed by you in preparation for the next day. This will help to identify the positive benefits of your digital detox experience as well as any negatives that you may experience during the digital detoxing process. Putting pen to paper to write up your daily diary entry, apart from being a much more connected and considered exercise, will enable you to chart your progress and provide you with invaluable feedback on your journey. The diary will also enable you to deal with any issues that arise, such as not being able to resist checking your smartphone or sending a secret email etc., which you may have encountered during your first digital detox.

#80
WAKE-UP CALL

One of the simplest and most important first steps to undertaking a digital detox is to buy an alarm clock. We like sleeping with our phones, it gives us a sense of being connected, and of comfort. It also stops self-contemplation, relaxation and creative thought. Checking our smartphones before going to sleep impacts negatively on our ability to sleep and the quality of that sleep. When we are stressed or preoccupied, the sympathetic nervous system responds by making our blood pressure rise, the heart beat faster, and muscles tighten. Looking at a bright screen, however small, just before going to sleep makes the body release approximately 22% less melatonin, which is the hormone that triggers sleep, and will guarantee a night of interrupted sleep. Digital devices should be switched off overnight or put on silent mode and plugged in to charge in another room. This prevents your smartphone from being the last thing you reach for before going to sleep and the first thing you reach for when you wake up.

#81
MY SPACE

Make a "go to" space that can become your special sanctuary. Creating both a physical and mental space for you just to be able to "be" will go a long way towards helping you to reconnect with yourself, friends and family and the natural world around you. Take some time to find a quiet corner and make yourself a sanctuary space to spend some scheduled uninterrupted time. It can be a comfortable chair where you can sit by a window for a while and watch the light change, or read a book or meditate. Once you have created your "My Space" make sure that you schedule in a time every day to spend an hour there, unplugged. Use that time as a positive step to disconnecting with the world and reconnecting with yourself. Give yourself time to be with yourself. Practice some mindfulness by listening to a favourite piece of music, fully focusing on every note; spend some time listening to the rise and fall of your breath; practise some gentle yoga or just rest your mind and body for a while.

#82
BACK IN THE BOX

Find a lidded box, basket or container and put it in the room where you have your breakfast or other meals. Find a place as far away from where you eat as possible, ideally near the entrance to the room and place the box there. This will become your new smartphone dock for breakfast and all other mealtimes at home. Before sitting down at the table, everyone should put their mobile devices on silent mode and place them into the chosen container and close the lid. Smartphones can then be retrieved from the container after the meal is finished on the way out of the dining area, ideally to be switched on once you have left the room. Try implementing this routine for 21 consecutive days at all mealtimes. By the end of the period, doing this at every meal will feel more normal than texting your way through a conversation. Discover the benefits of being offline and enjoying your food, being able to have "you" time and connect with friends and loved ones through having and being given absolute undivided attention.

#83
FRAME IT

Instead of reaching for your smartphone every time you see a special moment or an image that you would like to capture, try to capture and remember it, unplugged. Just immerse yourself in the experience by holding the moment and savouring the way it makes you feel by "framing it" in your mind and storing it in your internal memory card. To re-enforce the message you can even create a frame shape using your fingers, and take the equivalent of an imaginary photo which will enable you to engage with the moment fully and to remember it more accurately in the future. Sometimes just being alone with an amazing "moment" has the potential to be such a meaningful experience that it does not benefit from being immortalized for posterity by a digital device.

#84
STARTING BRIEF

In preparation for cutting back on your digital dependency it is important to establish tech-free zones at home. Try making parts of your home, which tend to be the hubs where people gather, such as the living room and the kitchen, unplugged, screen-free zones. The living room in most homes is usually dominated by a TV screen and is generally used as an "always on" background to "second screening" by family members using their digital devices while intermittently watching TV. Finding another place for the TV, perhaps in another room, den or spare bedroom, would shift the focus away from a media-dominated environment where family members gather to be "together alone" on their digital devices, and provide a tech-free environment for them to gather and communicate with each other in "unplugged" mode. If complete relocation of the main TV encounters too much resistance, a schedule of agreed digital downtimes and tech-free zones can be put in place as an alternative.

#85
IT'S A TURN-OFF

The relentless stream of notifications from social media, email and messaging makes it almost impossible for us to put down our smartphones let alone separate ourselves from them. In preparation for your detox, go into your settings on your digital device and disable alerts from all your apps, email and messaging. This will enable you, in the countdown to starting your detox, to start to separate and distance yourself from the constant pull of your digital device and regain control of the amount of attention you are willing to give to it, by checking emails, messages and social media notifications in your own timeframe. Stepping back from a fully immersive relationship with social media in particular will enable you to review your social media habits and gain a new perspective. This will also help you to establish whether the time you generally spend on social media platforms is productive and actually brings positive benefits to your life, or whether there is a need to re-evaluate your relationship and dependence on "being digitally needed" via constant social media and other messaging notifications.

#86
BACK TO BASICS

Preparing for your unplugged time during your digital detox requires forward planning. Make a list of the daily activities, planned excursions and programme of events that you will be undertaking during your digital detox and go through them individually to evaluate all the things you would normally use your digital devices for, such as checking a location with your GPS, checking the weather, getting a route map, your diary, banking, online recipes and your contacts lists, and make printed copies of them in advance. If you are planning excursions, get a compass and pull out that old box of maps and travel guides. Find your old camera and update the playlists on your iPod. Print related articles that will encourage and support your planned activities. Find old recipe books for some family baking time. Write down the key locations and contact information for where you are planning to go. Make arrangements to meet up in advance, agreeing the location, and make sure you are on time (the way it was always done in the pre-mobile age)! Apart from helping your digital detox run smoothly, time spent preparing the information to support your detox will also serve to engage you and get you excited for yours.

Now that you have undertaken the 10 pre-digital-detox prep steps, you are ready for your first digital detox!

A series of detox plans are outlined here, from a 1-hour tech-free taster for absolute beginners to the equivalent of a 7-day retreat, and everything in between. These practical steps can be integrated into your daily routine and can have a positive impact on restoring the online/offline balance of your life.

Following any digital detox plan will require a commitment and a readiness to deal with change. Change is not easy, but once you've chosen it, if you embrace it you will find that little by little, the rewards will far outweigh the challenges.

LEVEL 1

THE 1-HOUR DIGITAL DETOX

Plan to take one hour totally "unplugged" by putting your phone on to silent mode, in a drawer and left behind!

#87
WEEKDAYS

A morning run or gym session provides the perfect opportunity for you to place your smartphone on lockdown, leave it behind and revel in a tech-free hour where you can just concentrate on the workout. Your daily commute to and from work is another perfect time to be in the "moment" and focus on your journey rather than digitally multitasking by talking (hands-free) and driving or texting and walking. Being mindful and present on your journey gives you time to think, reflect on your day and arrive relaxed and refreshed. Lunchtimes are also the ideal time to go offline. Put your digital device in a drawer and let it go to voicemail. Amazingly, the world will survive without being able to reach you for an hour and you might just find that going for a walk, eating without looking at a screen, really tasting your food, and talking to a colleague while giving them your full attention, can feel surprisingly life-enhancing and fulfilling.

#88
WEEKENDS TOGETHER

As weekends tend to be more centred on the home environment, deciding to take a daily one-hour break from technology can become something that can be scheduled into plans for the weekend.

Unplugging with your partner, as a family or with a group of friends for an hour can be as simple as everyone "parking" their digital devices in the "special box" (see tip number 82) at the entrance to the kitchen, and cooking a meal or baking together, or writing a play or performing some music using instruments instead of an app, or even playing a board game (seems an archaic practice but never disappoints)! Finding new activities to make "unplugging" together a creative time can become something to look forward to.

#89
ALONE

Setting yourself a personal tech-free hour on each day of the weekend will give you permission to do the offline things you enjoy, the freedom of fully immersing yourself in whatever "unplugged" activities you choose, whether it is taking a long bath, going for a walk and really appreciating your surroundings, cooking something from scratch using ingredients you have specially selected, reading a book with actual pages that you turn instead of swipe, or just sitting in your favorite chair and listening to a piece of music, will go a long way to making you feel liberated and restored. You may enjoy your digital downtime hour so much you'll want to extend it!

LEVEL 2

THE 4-HOUR DIGITAL DETOX

By creating a personalized "unplugged" ritual even for a morning or afternoon, you are actually restoring structure into your life that previously would have been consumed and eroded by technology. Your tech-free routine can become a direct line to a more mindful and contemplative "you" where you can step away from your daily routine and connect more deeply with the internal narrative of your life.

#90
MORNING

Mornings are the perfect time to stay "unplugged" (assuming you have followed tip number 80 and have bought yourself an alarm clock). Your bedroom should be one of your sanctuary spaces and is the perfect environment to start your tech-free morning. One of the keys to getting the most out of your digital time out, particularly in the morning, is to get up early. Try and get up an hour earlier than you would normally. Once you have got over the "shock of the new" you will find that quiet, private, silent, distraction-free, uninterrupted time that is all yours is something to savour and appreciate. Early mornings are so peaceful, and it is the ideal time to meditate or write down some thoughts (using pen and paper), have a workout, go for a walk or run, or just have a long soak in a bath. Ideally a morning digital detox is not designed to be a time to catch up with work. This is space to be able to focus on your inner life.

#91
AFTERNOON

If in a work environment, start by sending out an email notification to colleagues and clients with an auto reply message saying that you will be "away this afternoon and will be picking up emails in the morning". Then switch your digital off and place your smartphone either in the specially designated container if you are at home, or lock it in a drawer if at work. Power down your desktop computer, laptop and other digital devices and put them out of sight or leave them behind. Go for a walk and really look at the natural wonders around you and if in an urban environment notice how the light falls on a building; engage your senses. If spending an afternoon unplugged together with a partner, friends or family, then share a coffee or tea or a meal and really talk, listen and fully focus on each other. An unplugged afternoon can be as full or empty as you want. You can arrange to be occupied for the entire four hours by organizing activities to avoid spending any "unplugged" time with yourself if that feels more comfortable at the early stages of your "unplugging" journey. Alternatively you can use those "unplugged" afternoon hours to power down and meditate, contemplate and reconnect with the analogue, quieter version of yourself.

LEVEL 3

24-HOUR DIGITAL DETOX

After undergoing a 24-hour digital detox you may have many mixed emotions. The relief and freedom you feel through periodically cutting the digital umbilical chord may ultimately turn out to be more addictive than your need to be connected to it. There may also be a euphoric feeling that you've tasted and been reminded of what it is like to really live and be present for a day, albeit tinged with the sadness of realizing what you have been missing. When you do finally log back on you will be surprised at how little you missed.

#92
PREPARATION

----

1 Pick a day that has some meaning for you like an anniversary, birthday or a landmark day, or if you prefer you can just select a day that works for you on a practical basis – like a weekend.

2 Let people know of your imminent "away day" from technology. Let friends and family know of your planned time unplugged and make arrangements to meet in advance of starting your detox.

3 The night before you start your 24 hours unplugged, switch off all your computers and digital devices and store them out of sight. Have a look at your list of personal goals and decide what you would like to focus your attention on. Double-check that you have everything that you need before you unplug. Print instructions, meeting points, maps, guides and whatever other tech-free items that you will need to make your unplugged day run smoothly.

4 Make plans, ideally in advance, of what you are going to do during your digital detox, so that you have a day of activities to look forward to.

#93
THE DAY OF

These 24 hours are determined by you and during this digital detox day you control your time, your attention, your thinking space and your focus. Whether you decide to go away or stay at home make sure you are fully present in everything that you do. The 24 hours of digital downtime can also be a gentle, meditative and nurturing time, depending on what your priorities and needs are at the time. Make sure to factor in some downtime and some "alone" time to give yourself an opportunity to slow down and give your brain a chance to recover from digital overload. If you plan to go on a trip for the day then try and include some "low key" moments amongst the physical activities. At the end of the day take some time to unwind. Create space to meditate, have a long bath to soak those aching muscles and read a book before going to bed.

LEVEL 4

48-HOUR DIGITAL DETOX

You will start to find that disconnecting for a weekend from technology is a nurturing experience. Enjoy the downshift in the pace of your day and take pleasure in no longer having to be on "read alert" as an instant-response squad to incoming messages; focus on just dealing with the now. View your weekend as a gift to yourself, a reward that delivers you back to yourself.

#94
PREPARATION

----

1   Plan in advance. This weekend should include some quiet
    time to be on your own, and quality time to spend with
    friends and family. Given that there are two days, alter the
    rhythm and intensity of the days so that at the end of the
    weekend you will have had both socially active times and
    more introspective moments that allow you to have time
    alone with yourself.

2   Switch off all your computers and digital devices and store
    them out of sight. Double-check that you have everything
    that you need before you unplug so there will be no excuse
    to plug back in.

3   Set up an "away" message on your email account, post
    a status to inform friends that you will be logging off. Let
    friends and family know so they are not alarmed and make
    arrangements to meet in advance of starting your detox. For
    emergencies let selected friends and family have a contact
    number where they can reach you.

#95
THE WEEKEND

Plan some family time doing the sort of things you did as a child: play games, draw pictures, go to a park, climb trees, play ball. Buying ingredients locally and preparing a meal together and eating it mindfully is a great way to connect with friends and family. Spend some time in the garden together or go for a walk in a park and really look at the trees and allow yourself to be fully immersed in nature's details. If you do decide to take a trip it doesn't have to be somewhere far away; it can just be somewhere local that you've never been to before and have always wanted to visit, or somewhere you know but haven't really taken much notice of as you were fully focused on your smartphone. The purpose of going tech-free for a weekend is to be in "the moment" to be really present and start noticing all the things that you have been missing while immersed in your smartphone.

LEVEL 5

THE 7-DAY DIGITAL DETOX

As with all habits your digital dependence is a habit that develops through repeated use. So, much in the same way, having spent seven days getting used to being separated from your digital devices can become a habit also. To make lasting change takes commitment, self-discipline and repetition.

#96
PREPARATION

----

1. Unplugging for a week takes planning. Often the best time to take a seven-day digital detox is to coincide it with a scheduled holiday or break.

2. In preparation for your week, switch off all your computers and digital devices and store them out of sight. Make sure that you really have everything that you need before you unplug so there will be no excuse to plug back. Print instructions, meeting points, maps, guides and whatever other tech-free items that you will need to make your "holiday" run smoothly.

3. Brief co-workers and ensure that they really understand that you will not be available. Set up an "away" message on your email. Let friends and family know of your planned time and make arrangements to meet in advance of starting your detox. For emergencies, let selected friends and family have a contact number where they can reach you.

4. Resend the notification message the night before you leave or start your digital detox just to remind everyone that you have gone "dark".

#97
THE "UNPLUG & PLAY' HOLIDAY

Make a programme of activities for both the mind and the body, to be undertaken both alone and together with family and friends. Plan to try and engage all your senses by scheduling some form of physical activity every day that activates the body, such as walking, running, swimming, yoga or playing a sport. Visit a local market or independent craft stores.

#98
SLOW IT DOWN

Allow some quiet time every day for some meditation, reading a book or writing some of your thoughts down. Make sure you factor some "slow" moments where you live more mindfully and notice the finer details of life, the people you are with and your surroundings.

#99
QUALITY TIME

Schedule some group or family activities where you are all engaged in an activity or all go on a day trip and can fully interact with each other. Spend mealtimes together really communicating and enjoying each other's company, and giving those you are with your full undivided attention.

#100
TAKE A PICTURE

Take some photos of where you are and the people you are with on an old-school digital or analogue camera. Get them printed on photo paper when you return home.

AND FINALLY...

Keep up the good work! This does not have to be the end of your digital detoxing journey. As we have seen, making small mindful changes in your everyday life can bring huge benefits to your physical and mental health. Re-evaluating and reassessing your relationship with technology will be an ongoing process as long as technology dominates our family, working and social lives. Remember you control your devices, your devices do not control you. Creating the time to reconnect with loved ones and ourselves in a digital free zone will have a positive impact on every aspect of your life.

CONCLUSION

So you have completed your unplugging journey, you may find yourself asking "What's next?" Now is the time to reset, tune in and unplug.

ALLOW THE NOW, ALWAYS

Unplugging is not so much a disconnection as a fine-tuning of our inner search engine. Practising moderation by finding a workable balance between our digital connectivity and our real-life connections is the key to establishing a new digital protocol where we can be fully present in our lives while using our digital devices as the tools they were designed to be. We accept that we live in a digitally dominated world that we have allowed to impact on every aspect of our lives, but although we are living digitally curated lives, ultimately we can't Photoshop our personality, or edit our souls.

We have to establish a new modus operandi of how to live with this new mind-altering, life-changing addition to our lives. Ultimately I believe that we know all the answers to the questions we want to ask, because they have always been there inside of us. We just need to create enough space in our lives and pause for long enough to be able to hear the answers.

We are living, breathing and extraordinary human beings with five senses, so let's find new ways to reconnect with ourselves by making space to be able to be fully present. By embracing rather than erasing solitude, we will be able to live a more conscious and mindful life where we can allow the "now", and through presence gift ourselves back to ourselves and to those who have a special place in our lives. We are here, now. Let's live the moment and rediscover the joy of mindful living in a digital age by finding a new way to reconnect with the poetry of life.

INDEX